JUST LIVE

A GUIDE TO PREVENTING SUICIDE

BY

DR. JEFFREY D. MORRIS

Words Matter Publishing
P.O. Box 1190
Decatur, IL 62525
www.wordsmatterpublishing.com

ISBN: 978-1-958000-82-3

Library of Congress Catalog Card Number: 2023946305

TABLE OF CONTENTS

I want to thank my dad, mom, stepdad, my children, my children's mother, my in-laws, and everyone who has ever supported me when I was feeling bad. I would not be alive today without all of you.

Thanks to instructors Dr. Derek Houston, Dr. Laurel Puchner, Dr. Dustin Foutch, and all of my fellow doctoral students at Southern Illinois University @ Edwardsville. Your support and encouragement over the last two years of writing my dissertation were the impetus for this book.

Thanks to Dr. Paul Quinnett from the QPR Institute and Dr. Thomas Joiner for always answering my questions. Their knowledge of mental illness and suicide prevention is and was so helpful.

I also want to thank all of the people who helped me write this book by offering encouragement, support, and even reading draft after draft prior to publishing. There are too many to name, but you all know who you are.

This book is dedicated to everyone like me who has dealt with pain so great that they thought about or attempted suicide.

Throughout the book, you will find places to journal and write your thoughts about your own struggles in life. My hope is that you might be able to share this book with others and help them find a way to live a long, happy life.

"People appreciate and never forget that helping hand, especially when times are tough."

– Catherine Pulsifer.

1. FOREWARD 1

by
BECKY PRINCE

I am Jeff's mom, so I have known him since the day he was born.... so I am a bit biased in my opinion of him. I knew almost nothing about depression and suicide until my precious son was diagnosed as being bipolar. The one thing I am certain of is that this disease is something that Satan himself created.

I was not aware of Jeff's struggles until he was well into his thirties. I do remember him isolating himself from the rest of his family when he was in middle and high school. But, I just wrote it off as being a bad day at school or just part of growing up. I really thought he was just a normal kid going through things that other kids go through.

Jeff became a teacher and got married to his now ex-wife, Kerri. They had two wonderful kids, and Jeff ended up getting a job as a high school principal. I remember sometime in the early 2000s getting a call from his wife, Kerri, and she said that something terrible had happened with Jeff..... it is still hard for me to say or type the words. Jeff had attempted suicide.

I know that Jeff has had other serious bouts of depression and attempted suicide multiple times. I also know that I don't know what all he has been through or even what it feels like to want to die.

Jeff has written this book to help others and offer encouragement to anyone who deals with depression or knows someone who wants to help a loved one. I have spent a lot of time crying and praying that Jeff would come to a point where he could find happiness, and I feel like he has gotten there.

Jeff is a very talented and intelligent man who has helped many people. He talks to people who reach out to him and teaches kids in schools how to help someone who they think is suicidal. He has really become a "counselor" himself.

I have learned that instead of worrying like crazy, I listen to Jeff when he tells me he is not feeling well and just needs space and time to work through his depression. I just back off and let him have time (and, of course, I pray for him every day).

Finally, I know he had to give up a career in education that he loved and thought he would retire from, but he has still made me the proudest mother in the world.

2. FOREWARD 2

by
STEVE MORRIS

I am Jeff's father, and I have learned that depression is a disease. It is not contagious, but it devastates families. I have watched my son struggle with being Bipolar for a long time.

I have seen him when he has been both severely depressed and also when he has been manic. There have been some horrific lows for him during the last twenty years or so. Yet, he still continues to face this challenge like the warrior he is.

He has dedicated his life to helping those who struggle with this horrible disease by teaching about how to manage depression in a healthy way and also how to help others who might be feeling suicidal. I love him so very much, and I am so proud of him for how he has learned to live with this disease.

It is my sincere desire that this book will be an inspiration to those who are dealing with depression or know someone who they want to help get better.

"My hope is that these words will remind you of the hope that lies ahead — and that you are not alone on your journey. Countless people have experienced this weight and made it through. These words are a testament to that."

— Anonymous.

3. INTRODUCTION

The first time I attempted suicide was on Friday, October 10, 1997. When I started this book, I could not recall the exact date. But I did remember it was on the Friday before Columbus Day in 1997. So, it was easy to look up.

It was a pretty typical day for me. I was married at that time, and my wife left about 7:15 a.m. for work at her elementary school. I dropped off our 7-month-old daughter, Chloe, at the sitter's and went to work at the Massac County School District Central Office. Kerri, my wife at the time, and I had been married for over six years, and Chloe was born on March 4, 1997. I had just gotten a promotion from being an assistant principal at Massac County High School to Assistant Superintendent for the Massac County School District. Kerri and I had also bought a beautiful home on the golf course just north of Metropolis, Illinois. Our life was just about perfect….. and I was miserable.

I knew suicide was a bad idea. I had thought about suicide many times before, but this was the first time that I knew I was going to go through with it. I spent the morning at work and went about my day like normal. I hated my job, but I was almost relieved because I knew that I would not be in pain much longer. This is a common feeling among people who attempt suicide. Feeling relief knowing they are going to end the pain.

I went home for lunch, shut the garage door, and left my truck running. I was in my truck with it running for what seemed like hours, but it was only about twenty minutes or so. After a bit, I could feel my heart racing at over 180 beats a minute (I have no idea why I checked my heart rate), and I was starting to feel sick. I am certain that I was only a few minutes from finally ending my pain and my life.

Then, I thought about Kerri and Chloe. I thought about the pain they would deal with and how sad my parents would be. I thought about Kerri's parents and all they had meant to me. For some reason, I turned off my truck, went inside for a bit, and then went back to work and finished my day. This is the first time I have ever told this story in its entirety.

I attempted suicide multiple times between the fall of 2002 and the end of 2010. Depression would cost me my marriage and my career, but it did not cost me my life. I am thankful every day for that.

In 2010, Kerri and I got divorced, and I left my job as a principal. I am happy that Kerri has moved on and found happiness without having to deal with my mental health issues. We have a good relationship, and I still love her as the mother of our kids. I am also happy to have come to a place of happiness in my life. It took me the better part of fifty years to come to a point where I liked myself and who I had become.

Some would say, "If this book can help one person, then I will be happy." I think that is a complete "B.S.!!!" I want this book to help thousands of people. Millions. If I only help one person, I am going to be pretty disappointed. In the end, I probably won't know how many people this book will help because it is hard to determine when you prevent suicide.

I do hope that after you read this book, you will feel like you learned something and want to use it to help others in your family, place, work, or wherever you see fit.

Throughout the book you will find places to journal and write your thoughts about your own struggles in life. I know that all readers will not choose to write or journal, but I added the journaling component (thanks to my dear friend, Kati Williams, for the suggestion) because:

- It helps the reader engage in the reading and reduces the monotony.
- Helps the reader think about how certain things discussed in the book impacts them (like coming up with your own plan for when you are feeling depressed or even suicidal).
- Increase recall on what has been read.

"If you're looking for a sign not to kill yourself, this is it."

— *Unknown.*

4. LEARN FROM MY MISTAKES

I have dealt with depression since I was in my early teens. I am not sure of exactly when it started for me, but I do remember being sad a lot as a kid and into my late teens. From the time I was in middle school up through high school and college, I was depressed a lot. I thought about suicide hundreds of times but never had a plan or attempted.

Sometimes, people like me are thought to have "just been born this way." Other times, it could be some situation that causes someone to become suicidal. I have never spent much time analyzing why I feel the way I do at times because I don't think it really matters. Even if I find the reason(s), then what?

For the purpose of this book, I want to talk about the most traumatic events I experienced as a child and young man. The first was my parents' divorce. Mom and Dad divorced when I was about six years old. My dad was about twenty-five, and my mom was around twenty-three when they divorced. They were just kids themselves when they had me. Their divorce was not that hard for me, but what was hard was only seeing my dad every other weekend and a month in the summer. I would cry every Sunday night when he would drop me off. I missed my dad terribly from the time I was six until my early teens.

I don't think it mattered which parent I was away from. If I had lived with my dad, I would have missed my mom just as much. I have a great relationship with both my parents and love them dearly. And I know they love me. My parents had a son before I was born. Stephen "Stevie" Morris was born on July 7, 1966. Stevie was about two months old when he was killed in a car accident. My dad was driving, and he was thrown from the car while my mom was holding him. Not long after his death, my mom got pregnant with me, and I was born on June 29, 1967, almost a year to the day of Stevie's birth. I grew up knowing I was special to my family because of his death.

The second most traumatic event of my life was my dad's divorce from his 3rd wife, Ann. Dad and Ann had been married since 1978, and I loved (and still love) Ann to death. She was a teacher at my high school and was great to me. They had my younger brother, Matt, in 1980, and things were great for me. When I got to high school, I had a great stepdad, John, and stepmom. I felt like a lucky kid to have four great parents.

In the fall of 1986, I was a sophomore at Rend Lake College and starting my second year of college. I was playing basketball and had a great freshman year. I was really feeling good about my life. Then, on a Sunday night in about October of that year, my dad called me to come talk to him at his home in

Woodlawn, Illinois. I met him at about 10 a.m. at his house, and he broke the news to me……he and Ann were getting a divorce. He told me why, but it did not matter. I was absolutely shocked. I had no idea there were any problems in the marriage. I was just sick.

I felt sad for me. I felt sad for Dad and Ann. Mostly, I felt sad for my little brother, Matt, because he was going to go through the same thing I had to go through as a kid at about the same age, and I would not wish that on my worst enemy. The rest of my year was awful. I was miserable for most of my sophomore year. It affected my basketball season and even my relationship with my girlfriend, who would eventually marry me a few years later.

What events in my life, if any, caused me trauma, depression, or suicidal thoughts?	Why was this even so impactful for me?	What have I done to deal with the trauma?

I left for Wisconsin for two years to play ball and go to school. Getting away from home was good for me. I grew up a lot from 1987-89 while I was away from home. By the time I returned home from school in May of 1989, I was a different person. I felt confident and happy, and I was pretty sure I knew what I wanted to do with my life….. marry my girlfriend, Kerri, and become a math teacher and basketball coach.

I got married on May 24, 1991, and got a job as a teacher and head basketball coach in Vienna, Illinois a few weeks later. Kerri and I moved to Vienna, and she eventually got a job teaching in Harrisburg, Illinois. My life was terrific, but I was still feeling depressed at times.

Kerri was supportive of me as I worked on my master's degree in Educational Administration. I eventually got a job as an assistant principal at Massac County High School in Metropolis, Illinois. In May 1997, I was promoted to assistant superintendent in the Massac County School District. I was not even thirty years old, and I was on my way to becoming a superintendent of a school district.

In spite of my professional success, my depression was getting worse. I was working in the central office at Massac County and missed being in the building with the students and staff. This was the fall of my first suicide attempt. Later in the year, I began to think that my depression was related to how much I disliked my job. I told Kerri that I wanted to get back into a job as an assistant principal. Although Kerri loved where we lived, she agreed to try to move to St. Louis.

In July 1998, we both got jobs in the St. Louis area and moved to Edwardsville, IL. I was hired as an assistant principal at Edwardsville High School, and Kerri got a job teaching first grade in the same district. Kerri and I had what seemed to be the ideal life…. Chloe was now three, our son Quinn was born in May 2000, we had a nice home, and our marriage seemed to be perfect.

I was still miserable. Even though I had not attempted suicide a second time at this point, I still thought about it a lot. I was really good at hiding my depression. Once again, I thought a job change would help me feel better. I was offered the principal's job at EHS and a job as an assistant principal at Oakville H.S. in south St. Louis on the same day in May 2000. It was a difficult decision, but I chose to go to Oakville.

By the start of the school year in 2000, I was working at Oakville High School south of St. Louis. It was a great job, and I loved the people I worked with. John Cary, the superintendent at the time, was a dear friend and mentor to me. Other than my dad, stepdad, and father-in-law, John was the most influential man in my life before he died in 2014.

The first time I ever sought help for my depression was in November 2000. We had a rally in the Mehlville School District for a big project that the community was voting on. It should have been exciting for me because we had worked hard to get this proposal to pass, and it looked very promising. However, I was becoming more and more depressed and starting to think of a plan to end my life.

I ended up calling our Employee Assistance Program to see a counselor. Over the next few months, I met with a counselor, and she diagnosed me as being "Bipolar 2." I was not surprised to have a bipolar diagnosis, but I had never heard of Bipolar 2.

According to Radack (2022), both Bipolar 1 and 2 are health conditions that cause extreme mood swings that include highs and lows. Both disorders tend to be similar in the severity of the depressive episodes, but the "highs" are different between Bipolar 1 and 2 (Radack, 2022). A person with Bipolar 1 will tend to have very obvious "manic" episodes where they spend money they don't have or go for days without sleeping, but a person with Bipolar 2 may just have trouble sleeping or feel like they have more energy during what is called "hypomania" (Radack, 2022).

Based on my history of ups and downs, I was certain that my Bipolar diagnosis was accurate. My low times were very low, but when I felt hypomanic, my symptoms were very subtle and hard for most to even recognize. And that included me.

By the fall of 2002, I was really sick. I had lost a bunch of weight and stopped sleeping. I had been hired as the principal at Affton High School in South County St. Louis, and I was terrified. I was like a zombie. In about October 2002, I attempted suicide for the second time. I tried to overdose, and

Kerri took me to the hospital when she realized something was wrong. She thought I was having a reaction to the meds that I had been taking. When we got to the hospital, I told the nurse and Kerri that I had tried to overdose.

Needless to say, my family was shocked. I had hidden my depression from them so well that none of them expected me to say, "I tried to kill myself." Even Kerri was surprised, and she knew I was seeing a counselor and taking medication. Kerri had no idea the amount of pain I was in during that time.

Over the next eight years, I attempted four more times and ended up in the psych ward at several hospitals in St. Louis. In 2009, Kerri asked me for a divorce, and I ended up losing my job in Affton. Needless to say, life could not get much worse for me. I was devastated by losing my wife and also my job. I hated my job, but I was embarrassed that I was forced to resign or be let go.

Kerri and I divorced in 2010. I did not blame her for wanting someone who was more stable. She stood by me for longer than she should have. In the end, our divorce was for the best, and we have done a good job co-parenting our kids. I am happy that she has found peace and has a great job as a school administrator in the St. Louis area.

Moving to Iowa

One of the most important things that happened to me was when Kerri and the kids moved to Iowa in the summer of

2012. I had given her the okay to move with the kids and decided to move myself. I was now working at home and doing some presentations on how to prevent suicide, so I was able to move to Iowa to stay close to the kids.

In September of 2012, I moved to Muscatine, Iowa. I only knew three people in Muscatine, and that was Kerri and my kids. Even though I was very alone, I never once second-guessed my decision to move. I could not imagine being a four-hour drive away from Chloe and Quinn.

During the first few years in Iowa, I spent my time counting the days till I could move back to St. Louis. I was not really part of the Muscatine community. Finally, in about 2015, I had an epiphany. I decided I was missing out on some good years of my life. I decided I was going to stop counting the days until Quinn, my youngest, graduated from high school so that I could move back home. That was the most important decision of my life.

I started bartending to get out of my house and meet people. I got a job as a bartender in West Liberty, Iowa, and loved it. I worked there for about two years and then took a job as a bartender in Muscatine. I absolutely love working as a bartender. Plus, it forced me to socialize and get out of my house for a few hours a week.

One of the most important things that changed for me in Iowa was I stopped worrying about the future and the next time I would feel depressed. I actually started to focus on enjoying each day. I have a tattoo on my upper chest that says "Vivere in momento," which means "Live in the moment" in Latin. I have it written in reverse so that I can read it when I look in the mirror to start each day.

By the time Quinn graduated, I was thinking of staying in Iowa. But I decided that it would be better to move back to St. Louis. Chloe was in school there, and Quinn wanted to move back as well. Plus, most of my family was within a ninety-mile drive of the St. Louis metro area.

My six years in Iowa had taught me a very important lesson. I was done thinking I could never be depressed again. I was now focusing on managing my depression rather than curing it.

Management vs. Cure

When I was in my late twenties and early thirties, I would get depressed quite often. When I would start to come out of a depressive episode, I would start to tell myself, "I am never letting myself feel depressed again." That was such a bad approach for me because I did not have that kind of control. It would be like a person with asthma saying, "I am never letting myself have trouble breathing ever again," after having to use their inhaler. It is just an irrational and unhealthy way of thinking.

Sometime around 2016, I changed my approach to how I thought about my depression and mood disorder. Instead of trying to prevent my down times, I embraced them. I could tell when I am starting to feel bad, and I changed my approach. I started telling myself, "Jeff, you have been through this thousands of times, and you will get through this period as well."

My whole attitude about my illness changed. I now treat my ups and downs as just something to be aware of and even tell people when I am feeling bad. Sometimes, telling my family and friends I just need to have a few days to myself, and I will be fine. I encourage people to check on me, but I will be back to my "normal" self in a few days. This change has helped me immensely.

Now, I just look at depression as just another part of me. It is not necessarily a great part of my life to feel depressed, but it is also not the worst part. My back bothering me is now much more of a pain to deal with compared to feeling depressed.

What are thoughts that I have when I am depressed that are irrational or unrealistic?	What are thoughts that I can use to replace these thoughts?
Ex: I am never going to let myself get depressed again.	Ex: I have been depressed before, and I have made it through that before. I know how to get through a depressive episode and will get through this, too.

Stop Worrying

First, I have to clarify this by stating that worrying can be hard to stop. Especially if you are suffering from severe anxiety. Telling someone who deals with severe anxiety to stop worrying is ineffective and cruel. However, I am talking about times when you are feeling normal and worrying about things like your first day on the job, a test, or telling someone bad news. With that being said, I come from a long line of worriers. My mother is a professional worrier, and so was her mother. Worrying is embedded in my DNA. Or, at least, it was. From the time I was a child through my early forties, I spent and wasted a lot of time worrying. I worried about Nuclear War when I was in junior high. I worried about disappointing people when I was in high school. I worried about being a failure as a teacher and school administrator when I was working in high schools. I worried about almost everything, especially when I was depressed.

Sometime in my early to mid-forties, I saw a great quote about worrying. It said....

"Worrying is like sitting in a rocking chair.....
It gives you something to do but gets you nowhere."

by Glenn Turner

That quote really strikes me as brilliant and helped me totally change my approach to "worrying."

Now, anytime I start to worry about anything, I ask myself, "Can I do anything about it?" If the answer is yes, I come up with a plan and do something to address it. If the answer is no, I move on.

For example, a few years ago, a very close member of my family cut off all contact with my parents, myself, and everyone close to them. At first, I was angry and then sad. Then I worried about him a lot. Then I asked myself if I could do anything about it, and the answer was clearly "No." I have not spoken to him in five years, and I still miss him, but I don't waste time worrying about him not wanting to speak to me or my family. Even though I hope he eventually allows all of my family back into his life, there is nothing I can do other than move on with my life and be ready when and if we are reunited.

What are things that cause me to worry?	What can I do, if anything, to help me reduce or eliminate worrying about this?
Ex: I worry about getting fired from my job.	Ex: I know that I am good at what I do, and my evaluations have all been positive. I know that I just need to continue doing the good work that I have always done. I can also ask my boss if there is anything I need to improve upon.

Support Plan

Another important thing that I did was create a support plan. Now, when I say create, I don't mean I put anything in writing and handed it out to people who help me. But I do have a simple plan that helps me when I am feeling depressed. My plan is:

1. I have people who check on me regularly to make sure I am doing alright. Especially if I have not texted or called them in a few days.
2. If they suspect I am feeling bad, they know they can ask me, and I will be honest with them about how I feel. I may say, "I have just been busy," or "I am kind of depressed."
3. Next, I tell them what I need from them. It is usually just, "Let me work through this, but check on me over the next few days."
4. If I am not feeling better, they remind me to call my psychiatrist to adjust my meds.
5. If I get to a point of feeling suicidal, someone close to me will come stay with me and make sure I am safe.
6. If I become suicidal, I will have them take me to check into the hospital so that I cannot try to attempt suicide and stay safe.

I have had this informal plan in place since about 2015 and have only made it past step #3 one time in the last eight years.

When I am feeling bad, I am pretty good at hiding it. I developed this skill through years of practice from the time I was about twelve until I was in my early thirties. And this is not a skill that is useful or healthy in any way.

One of the best things that happened to me was being able to talk to my family about what I was going through. My parents, in-laws, kids, and ex-wife have been so helpful in checking on me when I feel bad. It is very common for one of them to text or call me if they suspect I am feeling down.

In fact, one of the best examples of this happened when my son was living with me in 2020. I was lying on my couch, and Quinn walked by on his way to work. He stopped and asked, "Dad, are you feeling okay? You taking your meds?" I told him I was not feeling great but that I had taken my meds and would be fine. Before he left, I thanked him for asking me that and for checking on me. I have never been as proud of my son as I was at that moment.

If you believe that you need to create a plan when you are feeling depressed or even suicidal, use the form on the next page. You can use my plan as an example, but I suggest that each step you take gets more intensive as you move through your plan. For example, your first step may be to call your spouse to talk to them or have a safe person to go to at work. You should not necessarily start with checking into the hospital as your first step.

My plan for when I am feeling depressed is to:
1.
2.
3.
4.
5.

Self-Care

One of the things I tell people is, "Dealing with depression in a healthy way is simple, but it is not always easy." What I mean is that when I tell people what I do, their reaction is usually a bit of "That is it? That is all you do?" Like George W. Bush said, "This ain't rocket surgery!"

Even though what I do for myself is simple, it still takes work and discipline. Self-care is things I do on my own that help me feel better. First, I exercise. Working out most days during the week helps me feel better. I don't spend hours at the gym. In fact, I really don't like working out, but I know it helps me feel better. So, I force myself to get to the gym for about an hour (sometimes less) six days a week and get in a workout.

Something else I do is called mindfulness. According to the Oxford Dictionary of English (2010), mindfulness is defined as "a mental state achieved by concentrating on the present moment, while calmly accepting the feelings and thoughts that come to you, used as a technique to relax." Basically, mindfulness is a way of focusing on something you enjoy and distracting you from things that may be causing stress.

You want to keep the time you practice mindfulness short. I recommend under thirty minutes, and it can even be one minute. For example, if I am feeling stressed, I will set aside thirty minutes to watch an episode of Seinfeld (my favorite show). Once I start the episode, I force myself to watch the show without interruption and with my total focus on Jerry, Elaine, Kramer, and George. Once the episode is over, I usually feel a bit better and go back to what I was doing.

How you practice mindfulness is really up to you. You can do it by listening to your favorite song for five minutes or going outside on a nice day and just sitting on a swing and listening to the wind. It really depends on what helps you feel better.

Other things I make myself do when I am down are just getting outside, hanging out with friends who I enjoy being with, playing sports, spending time with my dogs, and watching a short show. I always enjoy the ones that make me laugh.

Find things that work for you and try to do them, even if you don't feel like it.

Finally, one other thing I do is give myself a break and remind myself that when I am depressed, I am not going to be able to give my full effort like I normally do. I may cut my workouts a bit shorter or just give myself a day to relax. Normally, I like to stay busy. But, sometimes, when I feel down, a good day is being able to get outside and get some fresh air. Remember, some days are like a plane landing.....if we make it through it alive, it is a good one.

List at least three activities that you enjoy doing to help relieve stress, anxiety, and/or depression.
1.
2.
3.

Meds and Counseling

It has been my experience that people tend to have a very negative opinion of mental health treatment for patients in the United States. I agree that it can be frustrating at times, but we have also come a long way in the success people have with psychiatric care and counseling and the overall attitude about mental illness.

According to Quinnett (2000), most people who die from suicide are not in treatment for their mental health at the time of their death. Even if you think some combination of medication and counseling will not be effective in preventing suicide, it is the best option we have right now.

My advice is very simple….. be a good patient, do what your doctors ask, and communicate with your doctors about how you are feeling during your treatment. I have talked to so many people who have stopped their counseling or medications after only a few months because they said, "This just was not working." I always ask them, "Did you tell your doctor your meds were not working?"

I have been on medication for over twenty years, and it took a while for me and my doctor to find what worked for me. However, I have learned to communicate about how it makes me feel the side effects, and I even asked if I could change meds that I did not like.

I also met with multiple counselors early in my journey to feel better. I used to tell people that counseling did not help me much, but that is not really true. I met with a counselor off and on from about 2000-02 and also during the time Kerri and I were going through our divorce. I learned a lot about myself. But, as much as I like to blame my parents for my depression (I don't really blame them at all), my issues were not their fault.

I think everyone in my family would admit that we were fairly dysfunctional in that I had multiple stepparents. But I grew up in a very loving family with parents and stepparents who have always been supportive of me.

If you have suffered severe trauma and think counseling can help you, I recommend trying it. Just don't give up if you don't feel a connection with your first counselor. If you don't like them, find another one. Keep searching until you find a counselor you connect with that helps you feel better. Finding doctors and other professionals who you trust and like working with can be a challenge. But the worst thing you can do is give up and not keep looking.

Have you ever met with a counselor before? How did it work for you? What do you look for in a counselor? What are your fears about talking to a counselor? Have you ever taken medication for a mental illness? How did it work? Did you communicate with your doctor about how it made you feel?

"Soak up the views. Take in the bad weather and the good weather.....you are not the storm."

– *Matt Haig*

5. WHY PEOPLE ATTEMPT SUICIDE

It is important to understand why people attempt or die from suicide. There are many myths about suicide, such as suicide being an act of selfishness or a result of poor mental health treatment (Achilles et al., 2004; Joiner, 2010). One of the leading researchers on suicide in the United States is Thomas Joiner. In his book *Why People Die by Suicide*, Joiner (2007) mentions that theories about suicide have been around for hundreds of years. Joiner (2007) points out that in 1621, Robert Burton wrote in his book *Anatomy of Melancholy* that suicidal people are unhappy, have always been unhappy, are incurable, and death is the only way to ease their pain. In 1897, Emile Durkheim wrote in his book *Le Suicide* that social forces like having values imposed on them had more to do with suicide than individual factors (Joiner, 2007).

Joiner presented his own theory about suicide in his book, and it is based on three factors. Joiner (2007) theorized that people become suicidal when two fundamental needs are not met: the need to connect with others and the need to feel effective or influence others. Joiner (2007) added that once these two needs are missing, suicide becomes attractive, and then it is just a matter of the person developing the ability to enact self-injury.

A common thing that people who have never dealt with depression will say to me is, "I just can't understand why someone would want to kill themselves. It does not make any sense." I totally understand why many people feel that way.

Suicide goes against everything that most people feel about living a long, happy life. Many people do things like get checkups with their doctor, get colonoscopies when they turn fifty, cancer screenings, eat a healthy diet, exercise, and other things to make sure they live as long as they can.

When I do suicide prevention training, one of the first questions I ask is, "Why do you think that some people attempt suicide?" I generally get the same answers….. a loved one dying, bullying, breaking up with a boyfriend or girlfriend, divorce, terminal illness, etc.

However, lots of people experience traumatic events like the ones listed above, and even though they are challenging, many people don't ever get depressed enough to consider or attempt suicide.

The reality is that people generally attempt suicide for one reason…. they want to end the pain they are feeling. My experience when I thought about suicide was that I was just in so much pain that I did not know what else to do. Dying was the only way I felt I could end that tremendous pain that I was experiencing.

> What are your thoughts after reading Chapter 5? Has there ever been a time when you felt suicidal? How did you feel? If you did not attempt, what stopped you?

"A person never truly 'gets over' a suicide loss.
You get through it. Day by day.
Sometimes it's moment by moment."

– Holly Kohler

6. WHAT HAPPENS AFTER LOSING SOMEONE TO SUICIDE

I believe that death by suicide is unique in how the loved ones who are left behind react. I cannot think of many other examples where the "survivors" left after death are left with so many questions. A few months before this book was published, I got a phone call that my cousin had died. For the first few days after Tracy's death, I was just devastated. He and I were the same age and were like brothers growing up. I was really depressed for the first few days after Tracy died, but after his funeral, I started to realize that I should not have been shocked by Tracy's death. He had been diagnosed with cancer about two years earlier, and even though he had gone through treatment to get his cancer into remission, I knew that the chances of him having a recurrence were pretty high. Although I was sad that Tracy had died at such a young age and left behind his wife and son, I knew there was nothing I could have done other than know that he was no longer suffering.

When someone loses a loved one to suicide, it tends to be much more traumatic. Trudy Carlson (2000) wrote about this in her book, *Suicide Survivor's Handbook: A Guide for the Bereaved and Those Who Wish to Help Them*. Ms. Carlson talks about how survivors tend to feel shame and guilt and ask, "If only I had done….." after losing someone to suicide.

First, she says that people who lose someone to suicide because they think they will be looked at as a bad person or that others will think something is wrong with their family. Second, they will feel guilt for not doing something to prevent the suicide. Finally, they will have "If only" thoughts like "If only I had not left them alone, they would still be alive." Although there may be some of these thoughts when losing someone to another illness or accident, the severity tends to be much greater when it involves suicide.

If you have lost someone to suicide and have experienced similar feelings, Carlson (2000) gives some suggestions on how to deal with these feelings in a healthy and effective way. Some of these include:

- Emotional Support Groups.
- Reading about others who have lost someone to suicide.
- Writing/Journaling about what you are feeling.
- Pay attention to your physical health.
- Do things that help you feel better.

If you or someone you know is struggling after the death of a loved one to suicide, I highly recommend reading Carlson's book. I have given several copies to people who have struggled after a suicide, and they have found her words to be very helpful.

If you have lost a loved one to suicide, how did you feel after their death? What did you do, if anything, to try to feel better?

"Suicide doesn't end the chances of life getting worse, it eliminates the possibility of it ever getting any better."

— *Unknown*

7. STATISTICS ON WHO ATTEMPTS AND DIES BY SUICIDE

I believe there are two kinds of people in this world when it comes to experiences with suicide…people who have thought about/attempted suicide and people who know someone who has thought about/attempted suicide. I also believe that the stigma attached to mental illness and suicidal behaviors is not nearly what people think it is.

I have spoken to hundreds of people about my experiences with mental illness, and I have yet to find anyone who has not expressed at least a little bit of empathy towards me. In fact, most people tell me about their personal experiences with either their own battles with mental illness or about a loved one who has struggled with mental illness.

Suicide will likely touch all of us at some point. As I said earlier, I have attempted suicide multiple times. Since 2010, I have known four people who I was close to who died from suicide. My uncle died from suicide in about 2014, and I also know of three former students who have died by suicide in that time.

Suicide statistics are usually about two to three years behind the current year because it takes time to gather the data for a given year. As of the writing of this book, the most recent data was from 2021.

According to the Centers for Disease Control (CDC, n.d., Suicide increases in 2021 after two years of decline), almost 48,000 people died by suicide in the United States in 2021. That is one death by suicide every eleven minutes. These numbers were similar to the all-time high of 48,344 who died by suicide in 2018 and 45,979 who died in 2019 (CDC, n.d. Suicide increases in 2021 after two years of decline).

Some additional data about suicide from the CDC (2021, n.d.) are:

- Suicide rates increased 37% between 2000-2018 and decreased 5% between 2018-2020. However, rates nearly returned to their peak in 2021.
- 12.3 million adults thought about suicide at least once in 2021.
- 3.5 million adults made a plan.
- 1.7 million adults attempted suicide at least once during the year.
- The highest rates of suicide occur among the elderly (people 75-84 attempt at a rate of 19.6 times/100,000

people, people 85+ attempt at a rate of 22.4/100,000), and people age 25-34 (they attempt at a rate of 19.5/100,000).

○ Although adolescents from age 10-14 attempt at the lowest rate (2.8/100,000), rates spike in the next age group, 15-24 (15.2/100,000).

○ About 55% of all people who died by suicide in 2021 used a gun.

○ Men die from suicide about four times more often than women.

Suicide among young people is also a problem. Even though it was stated above that rates are low among young people aged 10-14, there are some alarming statistics related to suicide among adolescents and young adults in our country. The JED Foundation (2022), a non-profit that works to protect mental health and prevent suicide among young people, found the following to be the case as of 2022:

○ Suicide is the second leading cause of death for teens and young adults ages 10-34.

○ Over 25% of young adults ages 18-24 reported having considered suicide within a month of being surveyed. This is higher than any other adult age group.

○ Almost 19% of high school students reported having seriously considered suicide in the past year.

○ 8.9% of high school students attempted suicide in the past year.

I believe it is clear that suicide is a problem in the United States, and it is apparently getting worse.

What are your thoughts after reading Chapter 7?

"Whether you think you can help to prevent a suicide or not, you're right."

– *Anonymous*

8. STRESS, ANXIETY, AND SADNESS ARE NORMAL...LEARN TO MANAGE THEM

After I got divorced in 2010, I tried a dating website. I had not been on a date with anyone other than my kid's mom in over twenty-five years, so I was a bit rusty and even nervous about starting over. I was looking at profiles for women on the site and noticed a common theme for many of them. Several would put a headline on their profile that said "NO DRAMA!" or something like that. I think what they really meant was they did not want anyone who was doing this to create stress or anxiety for them.

For some reason, that struck me as unrealistic. Life is made up of a great deal of drama. Hopefully, your life is not drama every day of the year, but I think we can all agree that we experience things that cause us stress, anxiety, and sadness at times. In fact, people we love dearly can cause us to have those feelings.

For example, my kids stress me out sometimes. I love both my children dearly, and they have both turned out to be successful young adults. But raising them was not always easy. My daughter was hospitalized with pneumonia when she was eighteen months old, and it was terrifying. Thankfully, she received great care and fully recovered. My son was an E.R. doctor's best friend. He was in the emergency room seven times before he graduated from high school with everything from a skull fracture to appendicitis. Although those were very stressful and caused me a great deal of anxiety and sadness, I found a way to get through it.

Life is a rollercoaster ride. There is a great scene in the movie "Parenthood" with Steve Martin where his character's grandma tells a story about going to the fair with her husband. She said he took her on the rollercoaster, and she loved how she felt both terror and exhilaration at the same time. She added that some people liked the merry-go-round, but that just went around and around with no excitement. Grandma liked the roller coaster, and so do I.

Life and relationships are hard sometimes, even with people you love dearly. We are going to have times when we feel stressed out, anxious, and/or sad. Breakups, losing a job, the death of a loved one, illness, and lots of other things in life are going to get us down. There is no way to prevent "drama" from happening.

My advice when I work with kids about preventing suicide is simple…learn how to manage stress, anxiety, and sadness in a healthy way. Find things that help make you feel better or distract you for a bit of time.

When I get to this part of my presentation, I ask kids, "What are things you like to do for fun that are healthy and legal?" They usually laugh, but I want them to know that looking at things like drugs and alcohol or dangerous behaviors to relieve stress is not healthy or effective in the long term. The kids usually respond with things like hanging out with their friends, playing video games, going fishing, and other activities that seem pretty innocuous.

I believe that the reality is that managing stressors is pretty simple, but it can be challenging. It is essential to develop those habits and practice them. It took me years to get to the point where I learned how to manage my depression in a healthy and effective way.

Here are a few simple things that I do that help me feel better when I am feeling bad:

- ○ Working out. Getting out and exercising is a natural antidepressant.
- ○ Going for a walk or getting outside.
- ○ Playing with my dogs. Pets have a great way of making us happy.
- ○ Being around people I like. Hang around with positive people and people who help you feel better.
- ○ Watch a show you like. Seinfeld is my go-to.
- ○ Practice "Mindfullness." It is a form of meditation. If you have never heard of it, google it. It is simple and can be very effective.

Trying to deal with the ups and downs of life can be a challenge, but it also is not necessarily that hard. Find what works for you and keep doing it.

What triggers cause you to feel stress, anxiety, and/or feelings of depression?	What are healthy ways you have/will deal with your triggers?

Other thoughts after reading Chapter 8?

"There were two classes of charitable people: one, the people who did a little and made a great deal of noise; the other, the people who did a great deal and made no noise at all."

— *Charles Dickens,*

9. MYTHS ABOUT SUICIDE

There are many things that people believe about suicide that simply are not true. For example, when I was a kid, people did not talk about suicide in public. If someone was depressed or suicidal, people would use euphemistic language like they were "sad" or just having a "dark time." If someone died from suicide, their death was usually put in their obituary as an accident or some other generic reason. People seemed to think suicide was a sign of being weak and mental illness was not real.

In the last few decades, mental illness has been dealt with in a much healthier and compassionate way in our society. It is my opinion that the biggest problem is getting people with mental illness into treatment because they do not have access to insurance, but that is a discussion for another time.

It is very common for people to tell me about their experiences with their own depression or someone they care about because they want to get help. In fact, not long after John Fetterman was sworn into Congress in January 2023, he checked himself into the hospital to be treated for his own depression and made the news public. I believe that his actions will go a long way to helping us do an even better job getting people treatment.

In his book, "Myths About Suicide," Thomas Joiner (2010) talks at length about several myths about suicide that he has found during his years of research on the subject. Some of the myths Joiner discusses are:

- ○ **Suicide is an escape, one that cowards use:** Suicide is not easy. In most cases, it takes a long time for a person to develop the capacity to attempt suicide. If suicide is easy, then why do 95% of people who attempt suicide survive?
- ○ **Suicide is an act of anger, aggression, or revenge.** Although suicidal people may be angry or irritable, suicide typically happens for one reason, and that is to end the pain.
- ○ **Suicide is selfish:** There is little to no evidence that suicidal people are more selfish than people who are not suicidal. In fact, my experience with feeling suicidal was that if I died, I would be doing my loved ones a favor because I would not be a burden on them anymore. People like me may view suicide as an act of unselfishness.
- ○ **Most people who die by suicide leave a note:** Most studies have found that less than 40% of people who die by suicide leave a note.

○ *People who die by suicide don't make future plans:* In 2017, Linkin Park frontman Chester Bennington died from suicide. Bennington was one of multiple Seattle musicians like Kurt Cobain from Nirvana and Chris Cornell from Soundgarden, who died by suicide in the last thirty years or so.

After Bennington died, some of his family members and friends were quoted as saying something like, "There was no way Chester was suicidal. I was with him that day, and he was happy and joking around. He was talking about the future just hours before he died."

When I read the comments about Mr. Bennington, it made me think about my own dealings with feeling suicidal. It is common for someone who has made the decision to attempt suicide to feel a sense of relief leading up to the actual event. I almost felt euphoric before I attempted because I knew the pain I was in was going to end.

Suicidal people may do "normal" things like schedule a vacation or buy a new car. They may act like everything is just fine the day that they attempt simply because they "know" all the suffering will be over very soon.

○ *You Can Tell Who Will Die by Suicide by Their Appearance:* Some people think that there is a certain type of person who will be suicidal. Some even think that things like money, success, fame, and other materialistic values will prevent depression. The truth is, none of those things matter.

Take someone like Robin Williams. There was not a more famous person on the planet than Mr. Williams. He had a successful fortune and was truly beloved by almost everyone. Think about it.....did you ever hear anyone say a bad word about Robin Williams? Everything I have read about his life said that he was very humble and kind and that the people he worked with loved him. However, he struggled with addictions for years and also with serious depression. He was diagnosed with Lewy Body Dementia, and he died by suicide in 2014.

My point is that suicide and mental illness affect everyone in every place in life. My experience was that my own success as an educator made me feel guilty about being depressed. I was a high school administrator at age twenty-seven, married to a beautiful lady, had two great kids, and lived in a big home with a pool. I felt enormous guilt that I was depressed and had so much to not be depressed about. I have learned that depression is just like cancer or diabetes in that it can happen to anyone, regardless of their place in life.

Some other myths that I have found in my time dealing with my own mental illness and teaching people how to prevent suicide are:

○ *If You Think Someone you Care About is Suicidal, Don't Ask Them About It:* Some people think that if someone you care about is suicidal and you talk to them about your suspicions, you are going to give them the idea to attempt. This could not be further from the truth, and I have found the opposite to be true.

I remember one of the first times I was in the hospital after a suicide attempt. I was released after a week or so, but my release required me to attend cognitive behavioral therapy every day for a few weeks. On the first day of therapy, I sat in my chair, and I was terrified. I was so ashamed and afraid. I did not want to be there, and I for sure did not want to talk to these strangers about how I was feeling. When it became my time to talk, I was in tears. I talked about what I had been through and opened up for the first time in my life about the decades of depression I had experienced. I immediately felt a sense of relief. I had lots of work left to do, but I took my first step to getting better at managing my illness that day.

○ *Once a Person Decides They Want to Die, You Can't Stop Them:* Suicide is preventable. Like any illness, there is no foolproof way, but you can prevent someone you love from taking their own life. I will touch more on this in chapter twelve when I discuss suicide prevention programs.

○ *Young People Are at a Low Risk of Suicide:* As I discussed in Chapter six, suicide is the second leading killer of young people. Suicide is not common among kids aged ten and younger, but it does happen. Once kids experience puberty and become teens, their risk spikes, so it is important for parents, educators, and others who work with adolescents to be aware of the risks they face.

○ *Suicide is a "White issue":* Some people think that suicide is more of a risk for white people. This could not be further from the truth. In 2019, the Congressional Black Caucus released a report titled "Ring the Alarm: The Crisis of Black Youth Suicide in America," and some of their findings were:

- ○ Suicide is increasing faster among young black kids compared to any other racial or ethnic group.
- ○ From 2007-17, the suicide death rate among Black youth increased from 2.55/100,000 to 4.82/100,000.
- ○ Black males under age thirteen are twice as likely to die by suicide when compared to black females in the same age group.

It is important to learn the facts about suicide to make sure that any assumptions you have are actually true.

Your thoughts after reading Chapter 9?

"Nothing exalts the soul or gives it a sheer sense of
buoyancy and victory so."
Each of us owes someone. We all benefit by reaching
out and helping others."

— Les Brown

10. WARNING SIGNS

One of the areas I talk extensively about in teaching people how to prevent suicide is the warning signs. However, I believe that most people intrinsically know when someone they care about is struggling. For example, one time, when I was coming out of a depression, my dad told me that he could tell when I was depressed as soon as he saw me. He said that I did not have to say anything and that my body language and the look on my face told him I was struggling. I doubt my dad could explain why he knew that intrinsically, but he knows me well enough to have that ability, and I believe most people can do the same thing with people they care about. Typically, when we help someone who is depressed, it will be someone we know personally. I think it is uncommon to notice someone who is depressed unless they are in a complete breakdown if their signs are subtle and you don't know them at least a little bit.

With all that being said, I am going to talk about four groups of warning signs related to suicide. You may have seen these in a different number of groups or presented in a different format, but this seems to work well in my presentations.

Verbal Warning Signs

When I talk about Verbal Warning Signs, I include things that people say, but also other forms of communication like writing, texts, and social media posts. The first type of Verbal Warning Sign is called Direct. Direct Warning Signs happen when someone is very clear about their intentions or that they are suicidal. This includes saying, writing a note, or posting on Facebook, "I want to die." It may seem too obvious, but it does happen.

The second type of Verbal Warning Sign is called Indirect. This type of clue is much less direct and may require some ability to interpret what the person actually means. For example, say you are at lunch with a friend on the Friday before you go on a break for a holiday. Your friend asks, "What do you think people would think if I did not come back to work (or school) after the break is over? Do you think anyone would notice if I was gone?" The person did not say anything that would be obvious that they are struggling, but it would appear that they want some help and that they may be in a bad place. Sometimes, it takes a friend or someone close to a person to reach out to and help someone who is suicidal.

Finally, sometimes people may make a joke about killing themselves. I know there have been times when something happens, like failing a test or getting a flat tire, and the frustration builds to the point where you might say, "I wish I could just kill myself!!" and you don't mean it. I tell young people that you may not need to take the person to the hospital because of what they said, but pay attention to other factors like their tone and if it made you feel uncomfortable.

If you think they are serious, ask them if they are suicidal (more about this later). One thing I add is that you should never joke with someone by telling them, "You just need to kill yourself." In about 2018, this was happening in quite a few schools I spoke in during that year. It typically happens on social media, and students would put "You need to kill yourself" in the comments for a social media post. Don't ever tell someone that as a joke. You have no idea how they will react to it, and you don't want that on your conscience.

Emotional Warning Signs

People who are exhibiting Emotional Warning Signs typically look sad, depressed, isolated, lonely, or like nobody cares about them. The challenge with Emotional Warning Signs is that they are hard to describe. I find it hard to describe what my son looks like when he is feeling down, but I know it when I see it. Very much like I described previously with my dad, knowing when I am depressed. This is where knowing the person well and caring about them personally is so important.

Imagine you are at school or work on a Monday morning after a weekend break. Your best friend comes in, and they just look like they are depressed. You know they are feeling bad, but you can't explain why you know it. I believe all of us have a close group of friends, family, co-workers, etc., that we are around regularly who we do this with. We can tell when people we are close to are in a bad mood when they are feeling happy, and when they might be suicidal. Make sure to use this intuition, and if you suspect someone you care about is suicidal, chances are they are just that.

Behavioral

The third category of warning signs is Behavioral. When someone is suicidal, their behavior tends to change. Some of the things a suicidal person might do include:

- Isolating themselves from others or stop doing activities they typically enjoy.
- Giving away possessions that they think are valuable or important to them.
- Doing dangerous things like driving too fast, taking drugs or alcohol, or anything where they could be hurt or killed.
- Changes in personality, sleep pattern, or attendance at work or school.
- Drop in grades.
- They are irritable, angry, or just don't seem like their normal self.

Again, some of these may be hard to observe, but you might notice them if they are happening with someone you are close to and know really well.

Situational

The final category is Situational Warning Signs. These include events or other things that happen to us that may cause suicidal thoughts. I have mentioned some of these previously, but some examples are:

- Going through a divorce. This can include not only the people getting divorced but also their children. Divorce can be very difficult, even if the parties know it is the right thing to do.
- Being diagnosed with a terminal illness. It is common for someone who is told they only have a short time to live to think about attempting suicide.
- Getting older. As mentioned earlier, the CDC (n.d.) has found that the highest risk groups for suicide are people 75-84 and people 84 and over.
- Owning guns. This is one that is very frustrating because, in the United States, we love guns. Estimates are that we have more guns in the United States than we have people. The Constitution makes gun ownership legal, and many states have very lax gun laws. Just

know that the CDC (n.d.) has found that over half of all suicides involve a gun. Make sure you are aware if you have anyone in your family who is a suicide risk if you have guns and keep them locked up and hard to access.

Thoughts after reading Chapter 10?

"Take the time to help other people without expecting
a reward or gratitude is definitely important in
living an optimistic life."

– Krista "K.K." Weatherspoon

11. PROTECTIVE FACTORS VS. RISK FACTORS

All of us are going to face challenges in our lives. Like my daughter told me when she was in high school, "Dad, life is not all rainbows and unicorns." As I mentioned earlier in the book, we need to develop good habits so that we can deal with stress, anxiety, and sadness in a healthy way.

So, it is important to know the difference between things that protect us from becoming suicidal versus things that increase our risk. Very simply, the more positive people, practices, hobbies, etc., a person has in their life, the less likely they will become suicidal. Examples of both are:

Protective Factors	Risk Factors
• Working out or exercising. • Have a support system. Know who you can talk to when you are feeling bad.	• Drugs and/or alcohol use. Many drugs prescribed for depression or other mental illnesses should not be taken with alcohol or other drugs.

Protective Factors	Risk Factors
• Taking your medication or seeing/communicating with your doctor, therapist, or psychiatrist as prescribed. • Attending church or being involved in your religion. • Pets. • Hobbies like fishing, hunting, or just getting outdoors. • Connections with people who make you feel better and can help you when you are struggling. • Having a positive attitude about feeling better. I don't like the saying, "Happiness is a choice." But trying to be happy is a choice. So, do things that help you feel better.	• Low self-esteem. • Divorce or a breakup. • Losing a job. • Graduating from high school or college. Yes, sometimes this can be a risk factor for kids because it is such a big step. • Moving to a new town or out of your parent's home. • Not having access to mental health services. This is common in rural areas of the U.S. • Experience some type of abuse. • Having multiple bad events happen at one time. • Terminal illness. • Getting older. • Having a negative attitude about getting better.

Dr. Thomas Joiner (T. Joiner, personal communication, May 8, 2023) adds that there is an asymmetry between risk and protective factors; risk factors can outweigh protective factors. When risk gets bad enough, he does enter protective factors into risk categorization, though he does use them as clinical leverage points going forward. According to Dr. Joiner, ominous risk is ominous risk, and protective factors don't seem to change that very much.

What are your protective factors?	What are your risk factors?
1.	1.
2.	2.
3.	3.
4.	4.
5.	5.

What can you do to use and even increase your protective factors and eliminate your risk factors?

"Remember, if you ever need a helping hand, you'll find one at the end of your arm... As you grow older, you will discover that you have two hands. One for helping yourself, the other for helping others."

— Audrey Hepburn

12. WHAT SHOULD I SAY (OR NOT SAY) TO HELP A SUICIDAL PERSON

When I was in my late thirties, I got my first tattoo. I did not even really want it, but I decided to get one (after a bit of encouragement from my kid's mom). Now, I have several tattoos. I have sleeves on my forearms, and most of the work has something to do with suicide prevention and mental health. Part of the reason I have them is to get people to start a conversation with me about their own experiences with mental illness.

When people ask me about my tattoos, and we begin chatting, they tend to tell me about a time they felt suicidal or when someone they care about was depressed. It is common for them to tell me that they struggle with what to say to someone to help them. First, I want to make it clear that I am not a counselor, and it is possible you are not either. So, if you have a loved one who is suicidal, at some point, you have to get them professional help. However, there are things you can say that can be helpful in the short term.

In fact, I don't think that what you say is nearly as important as your willingness to listen. Think of a time when you were feeling really down. Chances are that you felt really bad for a period of time, but when you had someone to talk to about how you were feeling and why, you started to feel better. It is likely your friend did not do anything other than listen. They did not solve your problem or say anything groundbreaking. But, allowing you to just talk and get things off your chest helped you be on your way to feeling better. Some examples of things to say and not say to someone are:

What You Can Say to Help Someone	What You Should Not Say
• I am here for you. • You are important to me. • I am going to help you through this. • I am not going to leave you. • Tell me why you are feeling bad. • I will go with you to get help. • Nothing (Just listen).	• Just get over it. If they could do that, they would. • Just be tougher. Depression is not a weakness. • Nobody said life is fair. • Stop feeling sorry for yourself. • I know how you feel; I have been depressed myself. Don't make it about you.

I want to add that one mistake I believe adults make when talking to kids who are depressed is that we do not always acknowledge that the reason they are feeling down is important. This happened to me when my son was about thirteen years old, and he had his first "girlfriend." She had just broken up with him, and I could tell Quinn was down. I asked Quinn why he was so down, and he told me that she had just broken up with him after he had bought her a gift.

Now, my initial reaction was to say something like, "Oh, Quinn, you will have other girlfriends, and this will pass. You will feel better eventually. It really is not that big of a deal." Fortunately, I thought about the time a girl broke up with me when I was about the same age, and I was crushed. I knew Quinn was hurting and that he felt like it was the end of the world. So, I asked him about her, and he told me why he was upset. We talked about how relationships can be hard and that breakups are even harder. I really did not do anything special other than make him know that I cared and was taking how he felt seriously. He started feeling better within a few hours.

My point is that adults have to stop telling kids that the things that cause them to be depressed are not serious. They may not be serious to us, but they are serious to them. Take time to listen and try to make them feel like you are taking their feelings seriously.

Think of a time when you tried to help someone who you thought was depressed or suicidal. How did the conversation go? What did you say to them? Based on what you read above, how do you think you did in trying to help them? What would you change, if anything, with your approach?

"When you feel like giving up, just remember the reasons why you held on for so long."

— *Unknown.*

13. HOW TO HELP A SUICIDAL PERSON: QUESTION, PERSUADE, REFER (QPR)

Preventing a person from dying by suicide is not nearly as difficult as many people may think. In fact, I would say that suicide prevention is simple, but it is not easy. Paul Quinnett (2000) posited that most people who die by suicide are not in treatment at the time of their death, and he believes that one key to preventing suicide is simply getting the suicidal person treatment. Quinnett (2000) added that although there are other factors to consider, like good self-management and sobriety, an individualized treatment plan is essential in helping a suicidal person get better.

Schools can play an important role in helping young people get help when they are depressed or suicidal. I was a high school administrator for fifteen years, and if I went back to that job, one of the first things I would do is have some type of suicide prevention training for students as part of the school curriculum. Many schools require students to take a semester of health, and I believe that is the perfect place to have the staff teach kids how to help someone who is suicidal.

I have seen some excellent presentations on suicide prevention. Usually, they are given by parents who have lost a child to suicide. These parents are to be commended for their attempts to try to help others and not have to go through losing someone to suicide. However, there were two things they would say that I believe are not effective.

First, telling kids that suicide is a bad idea. Of course, most of us know suicide is a bad idea. Even suicidal people know it is a bad idea. In his book *Cracked, But Not Broken*, Kevin Hines (2013) talks about surviving his jump from the Golden Gate Bridge in 2000. Kevin said that his first thought as soon as he jumped and was falling was, "I want to live." In fact, two thousand people are estimated to have jumped off the Golden Gate Bridge in an attempt to die by suicide (Hines, 2013). Nineteen of the approximately thirty people who survived the fall were interviewed after their jump and asked what their first thought was when they were falling. All nineteen said their first thought was something like "I have made a mistake…I don't want to die" (Hines, 2013). I knew suicide was a bad idea every time I attempted it, and I did not want to die, but I felt like it was the best thing for everyone if I just went away. Also, it generally takes a person a long time to develop the capacity to attempt suicide, and part of the reason for that is knowing it is a bad thing to do.

Secondly, they tell kids to ask for help when they are suicidal. The reality is that it is hard for a suicidal person to ask for help. Especially the first time. I can tell you that the first time I had to tell my family that I tried to kill myself was almost impossible for me.

When people ask me about how to help a suicidal person, I tell them that the key is to train the people who care about them about the steps to help them get help. It is kind of like CPR for a person who has had a heart attack. When you have to perform CPR on someone, they are dead. You are just trying to get blood to the brain until they can get to the EMTs and doctors so they can start their heart again. In the end, you are just buying them more time.

That is what suicide prevention programs should do... train all the students and staff how to help a suicidal person and buy them time to get help. There are multiple programs that have data to show positive results in preventing suicide, like Applied Suicide Intervention Skills Training (ASIST) and Ask, Care, Escort (ACE) Suicide Intervention Training. The program that I have used for over a decade is Question, Persuade, Refer (QPR).

In their book *Suicide in Schools: A Practitioner's Guide to Multi-level Prevention, Assessment, Intervention, and Postvention,* Erbacher, Poland, and Singer (2015) define suicide prevention as "any effort to reduce suicidal ideation, suicide attempt, and death by suicide" (p. 74). Erbacher et al. (2015)

described three suicide prevention models that schools should consider using based on the needs of their student population:

1. *Selective prevention programs* target students who might be at the highest risk for a certain behavior. For example, a school may use this type of program to help teen mothers or students who have one or more parents in prison.

2. *Indicated prevention programs* target students who may be exhibiting symptoms of a particular problem. This program might be used to help students who have reported suicidal ideations or previous suicide attempts.

3. *Universal prevention/Tier 1 programs* are used to target all students, regardless of their risk level for suicide. These are the most common programs used by schools in the United States.

QPR Training is a Universal prevention/Tier 1 program in which all the students take part in the training.

The essence of the QPR training I teach kids is:

- Stress, anxiety, and sadness are normal feelings and need to be dealt with in a healthy way.
- Suicide is one of the leading killers of young people.
- The warning signs for suicide.

- How to help someone through QPR.

  ○ Question: If you think someone is suicidal, ask them if they are. This may sound harsh, but I can tell you from my experience that being able to talk about how I was feeling when I was suicidal was a huge relief. I also know that "asking the question" can be difficult. It was for me when I first started teaching and using QPR. If you don't feel comfortable asking, "Are you thinking about suicide?" you can ask in other ways, like "Are you thinking about hurting yourself?" How you ask them the question is not nearly as important as just asking in some way to get them talking.

  ○ Persuade: Stay with them and ask them to let you help them get help. Offer to go with them to talk to a trusted adult.

  ○ Refer: Get adults involved so that they can get the professional help they need through a counselor, doctor, psychiatrist, etc.

There is much more to QPR than what I have listed above, but getting certified as a QPR trainer is pretty simple. I would recommend going to the link at https://qprinstitute. com/ to get more information. They offer support to anyone who wants to be a suicide prevention trainer.

Your thoughts after reading Chapter 13? How do you feel you would do if you had to ask someone if they were feeling suicidal? What would you say to them? If you have ever talked to someone who was suicidal, how did it go? What would you change?

"The purpose of life is not to be happy. It is to be
useful, to be honorable, to be compassionate,
to have it make some difference that you
have lived and lived well."

— *Ralph Waldo Emerson*

14. ONE LAST STORY

In October 2013, I got a message from a former student I am going to call "Barry." Barry was one of my favorite students that I had the pleasure of working with in my years as an educator. Barry was a good student, played soccer, and was just a pleasant young man. Everybody loved him.

Barry had messaged me late at night during the World Series between the Cardinals and Red Sox. He asked how I was doing and a few other questions since we had not spoken in a few years, and then he asked me if I had felt suicidal before. I knew at that point that Barry needed help; I just was not sure how sick he was at the time. We chatted a bit on Facebook, and he told me he had been suicidal in the previous few weeks. What I knew about suicide prevention through QPR kicked in immediately.

I found out Barry was visiting a friend and was about six hours away from me, so I could not get to him in person. He was also about two hours from home, so his parents would not be able to help him immediately either. I was able to get in touch with the friend he was staying with and told him not to leave Barry alone. His friend did everything I asked, and I also continued messaging Barry.

Barry told me he had a plan and had tried to attempt it before. A big reason for his suicidal ideations were some situations that were creating great stress and anxiety for him. I told Barry we needed to get his parents involved. He agreed to tell them the next day when he got home. I also messaged his dad and told him what was going on. His parents were both tremendously supportive and were ready to get Barry to a doctor.

Over the next few months, Barry was getting help. I did not check on him often, but I knew his parents were doing everything to help him. When I did message Barry, he sounded upbeat and hopeful.

Sometime in the middle of December of that same year, I was at dinner with my kids at Buffalo Wild Wings. I got a message from another former student that Barry had died by suicide that day. I was just devastated. I knew Barry was in a really bad place, but I was hopeful he would make it and learn to manage his illness.

After a few days, I went to Barry's funeral, and I met with his family a few days before. I spoke with them and told them that they did everything right. They were supportive and helped Barry in every way possible, but sometimes, people are just too sick to survive. It is similar to someone who gets diagnosed with cancer and does all the chemo and radiation and still does not survive. Suicide is the same way.

Barry's parents and I have stayed in touch over the last decade, and we have been a huge support for each other. In fact, Barry's dad shared some things with me that he learned after his son died. His dad said that he looked for a note, even though he knew not all people who die from suicide leave one. About a week before Barry died, his parents spoke to him about his depression. They felt Barry was very upbeat and positive as he talked about the last five years and his struggles. His parents thought he was getting better but would later believe that meeting with Barry was a verbal suicide note (indirect communication) that he was going to attempt suicide. He went out that night and bought a gun that he would use a few days later. His parents believed his positive attitude was really just feeling relief that he was not going to be in pain much longer. After Barry died, his dad searched his place and found something resembling a suicide not on his computer. The note was really a list that said something like:

- Debt
- Lack of money
- School
- Heartbreak
- Not wanting to get older and deal with problems.
- I don't want to survive this; I want to live, but not in a world like this.

I really believe that what Barry's family experienced is pretty common for people who lose someone to suicide.

You may wonder why I would tell a story about someone who died by suicide in a book about suicide prevention? The reason is that I had a lot of feelings when Barry died. I was very sad and frustrated and just grief-stricken, but I never once felt guilty. I told his mom, dad, and sister they should not feel guilty either. I spoke at Barry's funeral and told his friends and family what his mom, dad, sister, and I had been through with him and that although I was very sad, we had done the best we could, and he was just very, very sick. We knew what to do and gave Barry a chance. I take solace in knowing that I was able to help him and his family at least have a chance to help him get better.

My hope is that this book will help you and others in their search for ways to prevent suicide. About 40,000 people will likely die from suicide in the U.S. this year. About one million people will die from suicide worldwide. Hopefully, this book will help us lower those numbers in the coming years.

"Don't give up, don't ever give up."

– Jim Valvano

15. ABOUT THE AUTHOR

Jeff Morris currently lives in St. Louis with his dog, Griff. He has two children, Chloe (26) and Quinn (23), who also live in St Louis.

Jeff has spent the last decade teaching people how to help someone they think is suicidal using QPR. He cannot recommend strongly enough that every school should have some type of suicide prevention training for their students and staff.

Other Resources

- If you ever lose a student to suicide, this is a great resource for planning how to deal with it at your school. https://sprc.org/online-library/after-suicide-toolkit-schools
- If you are interested in learning about someone who has lost someone to suicide, watch the documentary "Boy Interrupted." This documentary is a powerful story about the life and suicide of Evan Perry. His parents, Dana and Hart Perry are documentarians and

use their stories about Evan, as well as stories from his friends and family, to help others understand how a person so young can die from suicide, even when he has a great support system around him. You can find the documentary at https://www.youtube.com/watch?v=Xh6ix0PZ8UQ

- www.suicidology.org (American Association of Suicidology)
- www.afsp.org (American Foundation for Suicide Prevention)
- www.cdc.gov (Centers for Disease Control)
- www.nami.org (National Alliance for the Mentally Ill)
- www.nimh.nih.gov (National Institute for Mental Health)

If you or someone you care about is feeling suicidal, please call the National Suicide Hotline at 1-800-273-8255 or use the new Crisis Lifeline #988.

I hope this book and the information in it is useful for you. If I can ever help in any way, please email me at jdmoe67@gmail.com. Peace.

REFERENCES

Achilles, J., Gray, D. & Moskos, M. A. (2004). Adolescent suicide myths in the United States. *Crisis, 25*(4), 176-182.

Carlson, T. (2000). *Suicide survivors' handbook: a guide for the bereaved and those who wish to help them.* Benline Press.

Centers for Disease Control. (n.d). Suicide increases in 2021 after two years of decline. https://www.cdc.gov/nchs/ pressroom/nchs_press_releases/2022/20220930.htm

Emergency Taskforce on Black Youth Suicide and Mental Health. (2019). *Ring the alarm: The crisis of black youth suicide in America.* National Action Alliance for Suicide Prevention. https://theactionalliance.org/resource/ ring-alarm-crisis-black-youth-suicide-america

Hines, K. (2013). *Cracked, not broken.* Rowman & Littlefield Publishers, Inc.

JED Foundation. (2022). Mental health and suicide statistics. https://jedfoundation.org/mental-health-and-suicide-statistics

Joiner, T. (2007). *Why people die by suicide.* Harvard University Press.

Joiner, T. (2010). *Myths about suicide.* Harvard University Press.

"Mindfulness." Oxford Dictionary of English, edited by Angus Stevenson, Oxford English Press. (2010).

Quinnett, P. (2000). *Counseling people with suicide.* The QPR Institute Inc.

Radack, J. (2022, March 29). *Understanding bipolar disorder.* MayoClinicPress. https://mcpress.mayoclinic.org/women-health/understanding-bipolar-disorder/?mc_id=global&utm_source=webpage&utm_medium=l&utm_content=epsmentalhealth&utm_campaign=mayoclinic&geo=global&placementsite=enterprise&invsrc=other&cauid=177193

www.ingramcontent.com/pod-product-compliance
Lightning Source LLC
Chambersburg PA
CBHW071210120626
46546CB00006B/2500